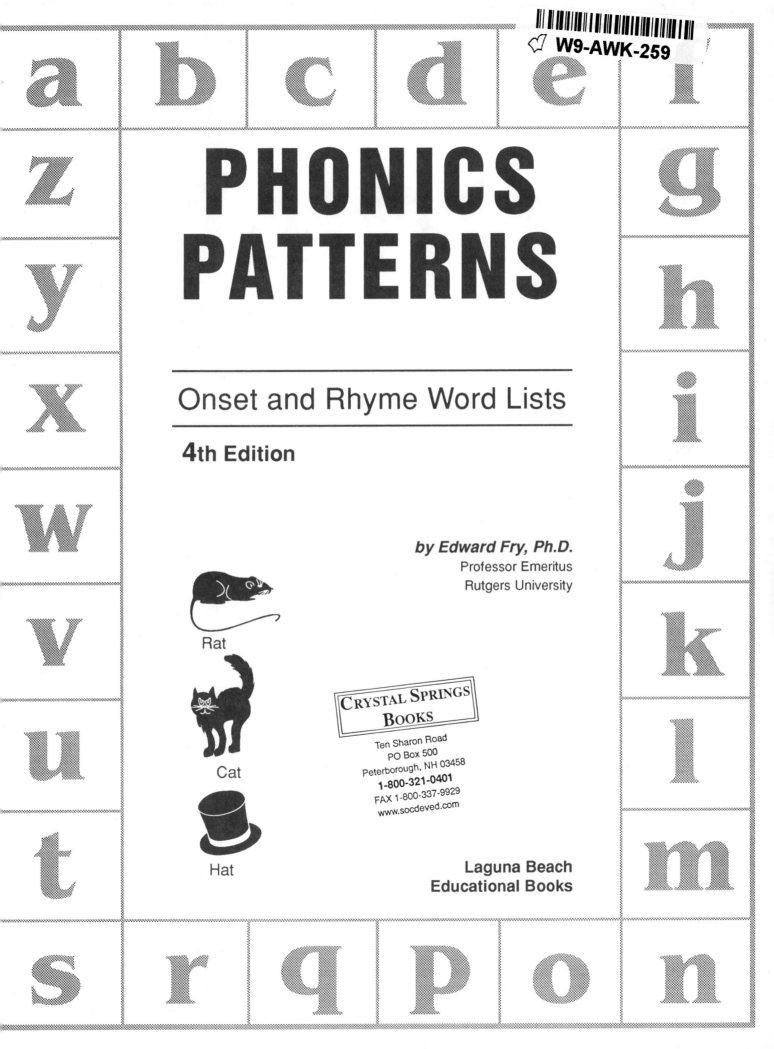

# PHONICS PATTERNS

## Onset and Rhyme Word Lists

**4**th Edition

*by Edward Fry, Ph.D.*
Professor Emeritus
Rutgers University

Rat

Cat

Hat

CRYSTAL SPRINGS
BOOKS

Ten Sharon Road
PO Box 500
Peterborough, NH 03458
**1-800-321-0401**
FAX 1-800-337-9929
www.socdeved.com

Laguna Beach
Educational Books

W9-AWK-259

**PHONICS PATTERNS**
**Onset and Rhyme Word Lists**
**4th Edition**

**Laguna Beach Educational Books**
245 Grandview
Laguna Beach, CA 92651
Ph: (714) 494-4225  Fax: (714) 494-2403
E-mail orders & Website: www.lagunabooks.com


Fourth Edition

Copyright © 1998
by Edward Fry
Printed in the United States of America
by Media Lithographics, Los Angeles, CA
Edited by Reta Holmback
Typography by Pen & Palette


ISBN 0-87673-026-8

# Table of Contents

**Phonics Discussion** . . . . . . . . . . . . . . . . . . . . . . . . . . . . . . . . . . . .5-6

**Teaching Suggestions** . . . . . . . . . . . . . . . . . . . . . . . . . . . . . . .7-10

**Getting Technical** . . . . . . . . . . . . . . . . . . . . . . . . . . . . . . . . . . . .11

**Rhyme Patterns**

**A**
Short A Sound . . . . . . . . . . . . . . . . . . . . . . . . . . . . . . .12-15

Long A Sound . . . . . . . . . . . . . . . . . . . . . . . . . . . . . . . .16-18

Broad A Sound . . . . . . . . . . . . . . . . . . . . . . . . . . . . . . .19

**E**
Short E Sound . . . . . . . . . . . . . . . . . . . . . . . . . . . . . . . .20-23

Long E Sound . . . . . . . . . . . . . . . . . . . . . . . . . . . . . . . .24-26

**I**
Short I Sound . . . . . . . . . . . . . . . . . . . . . . . . . . . . . . . . .27-30

Long I Sound . . . . . . . . . . . . . . . . . . . . . . . . . . . . . . . . .31-33

**O**
Short O Sound . . . . . . . . . . . . . . . . . . . . . . . . . . . . . . .34-35

Long O Sound . . . . . . . . . . . . . . . . . . . . . . . . . . . . . . . .36-38

Short OO Sound . . . . . . . . . . . . . . . . . . . . . . . . . . . . . .39

Long OO Sound . . . . . . . . . . . . . . . . . . . . . . . . . . . . . .40-42

Broad O Sound . . . . . . . . . . . . . . . . . . . . . . . . . . . . . . .43-45

OI Sound . . . . . . . . . . . . . . . . . . . . . . . . . . . . . . . . . . . . .46

OU Sound . . . . . . . . . . . . . . . . . . . . . . . . . . . . . . . . . . . .47-48

**U**
Short U Sound . . . . . . . . . . . . . . . . . . . . . . . . . . . . . . . .49-52

UR Sound . . . . . . . . . . . . . . . . . . . . . . . . . . . . . . . . . . . .53-54

**Diagnostic Test** . . . . . . . . . . . . . . . . . . . . . . . . . . . . . . . . . . . .55-56

**Phonics Charts** . . . . . . . . . . . . . . . . . . . . . . . . . . . . . . . . . . . .57-60

**100 Instant Words** . . . . . . . . . . . . . . . . . . . . . . . . . . . . . . . . .61-62

**Index of Rhyme Patterns** . . . . . . . . . . . . . . . . . . . . . . . . . . .63

**Suggested Teaching Order** . . . . . . . . . . . . . . . . . . . . . . . . . .64

Note: Rhymes (vowel sound plus consonant pattern) are alphabetical within the above vowel sound groups. For alphabetical listing of rhymes see 63.

# Preface

This is both a new and an old approach to teaching phonics for reading instruction.

You can call these lists "phonograms" or "word families" if you are more comfortable with those terms.

It is old because for decades teachers have been teaching "phonograms" or "word families". They teach them as part of games or devices like word wheels. They teach them more formally as word lists on chalkboards or on charts. They are the basis of many worksheets. And they are used as very informal or incidental instruction. For example, when a student has trouble sounding out an unknown word which contains a phonogram, the teacher not only points out the phonogram but also shows several other words that contain the same pattern.

Phonogram word lists were used in the New England Primer and Webster's Blue Back Spelling Books several centuries ago, so we don't claim that they are a new idea. But we do claim that these lists are refined, updated, expanded and more accurate in vowel pronunciation. In fact, this is the biggest, most complete listing of phonograms in existence.

Well, so what is new? For one thing the terminology is new. The terms "onset" and "rhyme" are used by linguists because they illustrate something basic about a syllable. So while most of the lists look exactly like phonograms, let's explore the onset and rhyme concept.

First of all a syllable is defined as a vowel sound (vowel phoneme) with or without attached consonants. Most syllables have a consonant sound at the beginning and a consonant sound at the end, with a vowel in the middle. However, you can omit one or both consonants. For example, "go" has no terminal consonant and it is both a word and a syllable; the final "O" in "po-li-o" has neither an onset nor an end consonant sound.

Also, the beginning consonant sound may actually be a blend of 2 or 3 consonant sounds (ex., "stop"). Linguists call this beginning consonant sound "onset" and the following vowel or vowel plus end consonant "rhyme".

| WORD | | ONSET | | RHYME |
|------|---|-------|---|-------|
| CAT | = | C | + | AT |
| BLACK | = | BL | + | ACK |
| GO | = | G | + | O |

Furthermore, they have identified that the break between the onset and the rhyme is a much more natural break than a break between the vowel and the end consonant. So there is at least a theoretical justification for analyzing syllables into an onset and rhyme division rather than in breaking up the syllable into individual phonemes. In classroom practice many teachers agree, and this probably accounts for the teaching of phonograms down through the decades.

The word lists in this book contain only one syllable words; however, there are many polysyllabic words that contain the same onset and rhyme patterns. For example, note the -ink in "think" and "unthinkable" or the -in in "begin".

Other new terminology might discuss rhymes as "spelling patterns", which is also correct. Some people don't like the idea of teaching single phoneme phonics (C+A+T) and prefer to talk about patterns like the "AT" found in C+AT and H+AT and the changing consonant as "consonant substitution". A related term to pattern is "letter cluster", although a letter cluster often refers to several sounds found together on many occasions. Examples are blends like "BL" or "ST".

So there are a number of ways of analyzing written language. Classroom teachers, however, can stand only so much theorizing and terminology changes. After that they have to teach students to read and spell. These word lists of rhymes (word families) may help. Use them any way you wish.

# Phonics Discussion

Some teachers, tutors, or parents who use this book would like a bit of information about "phonics". If that sounds like you, here goes:

There are two main systems of writing. Most languages use an alphabet. This means a set of symbols that more or less represent speech sounds. English falls into this category.

A few languages use ideograph symbols. This means that the symbol stands for the concept. Chinese falls into this category. Hence, a person who lives in south China cannot call up someone who lives in north China because they speak a different language, but they can write letters to each other or read the same newspaper. One problem with the ideograph system of writing is that it is difficult to learn and takes a lot of school time. Alphabetic languages are easier to learn to read and write.

Now, English, our language, uses an alphabet (set of symbols) that was designed for another language (Latin). The match between the written letter and spoken sound is not too good because spoken English has changed over the centuries.

Another problem is that many words used in English come from other languages with variant spellings or use of symbols.

However, despite all this, there is still a good bit of correspondence between the spoken sound and the written symbol. Trying to teach and understand this is what teachers call phonics. Linguists call it phoneme-grapheme correspondence. Phonics is taught as part of reading lessons to help students "sound out" unknown words, and it is taught as part of spelling lessons to help students correctly write words that they are learning.

Traditional, and the most common, phonics teaching tends to follow the method of individual sound connected to its spelling. Each sound in the word is taught. For example, "cat" has 3 sounds, /k/, /a/, /t/, and "boy" has 2 sounds, /b/ and /oi/. Our other phonics book called Phonics Charts, A Complete Phonics Curriculum on 99 Charts, is based on "phoneme–grapheme correspondence". For example, one chart teaches that the letter C makes the /k/ sound with 10 example words. Another chart teaches the /a/ sound, and another teaches the /t/ sound.

Phonics Patterns teaches another approach to phonics. This book contains phonics patterns or certain combinations of letters that make certain sounds. More specifically it contains onset and rhyme patterns. As was mentioned in the preface, the onset is the beginning consonant sound(s) and the rhyme is the following vowel plus consonant sounds. An example of a phonics pattern is, "cat, hat, sat, etc.", or "boy, toy, etc.".

While these patterns are not a complete course in phonics, they are a highly effective way of teaching a lot of phonics knowledge. Furthermore, they are in harmony with virtually any single sound phonics system so that they can supplement almost any kind of phonics instruction. These patterns teach a lot about single consonant sounds and various vowel sound spellings.

For very young students, such as preschoolers or kindergartners, or adults who may have never had any reading instruction in English, these patterns also enhance something called "phoneme awareness". This means the internal realization that words are made up of discrete and interchangeable sounds. Phoneme awareness might also be thought of as readiness for learning how to read, or readiness for more formal phonics instruction.

At first learning phonics might seem like a very difficult job. In English there are somewhere between 39 and 44 different sounds (phonemes), depending on which linguist or which dictionary you are using as an authority. And these some 40 odd sounds are spelled (written) using several hundred different letter combinations. For example, the Long A sound is spelled AI in "aid", and A-E in "made", or AY in "say".

However, most people do learn a good bit of phonics, whether it is taught formally or not, because phonics patterns are so prevalent in the English writing (spelling) system. But many teachers and educational researchers have found that the teaching of phonics, particularly with beginning readers and writers, does facilitate learning how to read and how to spell.

So in that spirit, I offer you some raw material for teaching phonics – the over 340 phonics patterns found in this book.

If you would like to see a more complete phonics system, a traditional phonics (or phoneme grapheme system) of both common and uncommon correspondences, study the charts in the Appendix. Most of those correspondences are illustrated with real words in the phonics patterns in this book.

Good luck with your teaching, and if you haven't already done so, look over the section following this preface on Teaching Suggestions.

*"Skilled readers look at letters and see patterns."*

Marilyn Adams
Author of Beginning to Read,
MIT Press

*"There is a well established relationship between phonological awareness and reading achievement."*

Baker, Serpek & Sonnenschein
National Reading Research Center

*"Phonics instruction needs to include the teaching of onsets and rhymes."*

Jo Anne Vacca, Richard Vacca & Mary Grove
Learning to Read, Harper Collins

# Teaching Suggestions

This book is a "teacher's tool". It is raw material to be included as part of a reading lesson or a spelling lesson. Reading and spelling lessons are sometimes interchangeable – one helps the other and vice versa. So teachers can use these phonics patterns any way they wish: direct formal instruction, incidental learning, supplemental to other lessons in phonics or even for speech correction.

This material is useful for teaching elementary children, remedial secondary, ESL (English as a Second Language), or adult literacy instruction

## Which Do You Teach First?

Which rhyme lists do you teach first? For example, do you teach "-ab, cab, dab, gab", the first one in the book? Or do you teach all the short vowels first? There are several good answers:

(1) On the last page of this book is a list of rhymes (phonogram families) that are ranked by the number of example words. For example, the rhyme -AY can form a whopping 26 different words just by changing the beginning consonant sound(s), and the first 5 rhymes form the basis of over a hundred different words. This shows some of the efficiency of using the phonics patterns in this book as one way to increase reading and spelling vocabulary.

(2) Another way to organize your teaching is to use these patterns to illustrate phonics rules. You might notice in this edition we have added phonics rules like the Final E Rule or Vowel Digraphs explanations where appropriate at the beginning page of each vowel sound. As a general principle we suggest you teach short vowels before long vowels and long vowels before other vowel sounds.

(3) These phonics patterns are also very useful in incidental teaching. For example, if you wish to drive home a point about a word in your spelling lesson or a new word in a reading lesson, extend the lesson by showing other words in the same pattern. For example, if a student can't read or spell "late", help him to sound it out and show a number of other words in the "-ate" family.

(4) Remember, there is a Phonics Pattern Diagnostic Test in the Appendix should you care to use it for suggestions on what needs teaching. Here are some different types of lessons you can try with these phonics patterns:

## Make Charts

| -ab | -ag |
|-----|-----|
| cab | bag |
| dab | gag |
| gab | lag |
| jab | jag |

Every day put a different list or two on the chalkboard or chart. Sometimes let a student write the list on the board or make the chart. Have the class as a whole or small groups read the list. Discuss the words by using them in a sentence or say something about their meaning. Feel free to omit obscure or unsuitable words; the purpose is to learn the pattern (rhyme) and to learn the use of different consonants.

You can select list patterns to tie in with your other spelling or reading lessons. Don't do too many at one time. For young children or beginning adults, do only one or two.

You can select lists in any order. For example, some teachers may wish to do all the Short Vowels first, then the Long Vowels. Others might choose to do all the easy A groups, then later select less common or harder groups. These groups also can nicely

## Individual Lists

In tutoring situations or in whole class situations, have the student write his or her own list for study. You can also duplicate a page of this book for individual study in class or for homework. In school or in adult literacy situations, let one student teach another — it helps them both.

## Spelling Lessons

These lists are ideal for spelling lessons. A student might complain when you say that they must have 20 words on a spelling test, but when they find out that half the words fall into a pattern of -ack like "back, hack, Jack, etc." and the other half follow a similar pattern, their anxiety is eased. Phonics spelling lessons like these are only one aspect of spelling instruction. If you want to see a more complete spelling program that also includes high frequency (often non-phonetic) words, homophones, suffixes, and much more, see the Spelling Books listed inside the back cover.

## Cards

An easy type of card to make is to put all the onsets (beginning consonants) on small cards, and a number of copies of the rhyme on other cards. The student tries to match cards to make real words. Mix several groups together to make it harder or add more onsets than make real words.

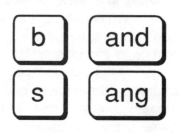

If you want to get a bit fancy, use one color card or one color marker ink for onsets and a different color for rhymes.

These cards can also be used to make a game; students take turns drawing cards from a pile and when they get two that make a real word, they get a point.

## Word Wheels and Slip Charts

Word wheels have the rhyme printed on the smaller top wheel and the larger wheel behind it has different onsets printed around the edge. By turning the larger wheel, different words are formed. Students often like this unique presentation and it provides some repetitive practice which aids learning.

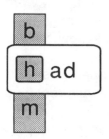

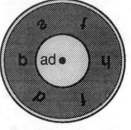

Slip charts are similar to word wheels except instead of being round they are long and narrow. Put the rhyme on the top card and cut a slot beside it. Put the onsets on a narrower strip and slide it past the opening in the top chart to make a word.

## Write a Poem

Dr. Seuss long ago discovered that children like poems that have end rhymes. If you don't have The Cat In The Hat in your classroom, run to the nearest library and borrow a copy.

See what your students can do with some pattern like -ay and words like May, jay, day, etc. Should you want to do a little advanced teaching, you might point out that -ey has the same sound as in "grey" and "they".

Seek out some good poetry examples from your reading textbook or a poetry anthology for children. Your librarian can help you.

## Stink Pinks

Do you never tell jokes or have fun with words in your class? Dullsville. Try getting your students to develop some stink pinks using phonics patterns. A stink pink is a rhyming pair of words in answer to a question. *For example:*

| | |
|---|---|
| What is an overweight feline? | A fat cat. |
| What is a strange rabbit? | A rare hare. |

Again, you can mix pattern families to illustrate similar sounds:

| | |
|---|---|
| What is the most important airplane? | The main plane. |

Well, these are not too good, but you get the idea. And you and your students can do better.

## Phoneme Awareness

A very important part of phonics teaching is for the student to realize that words are made up of specific sounds (phonemes). Furthermore, that these same few sounds come up in many different words. And finally (this is phonics), that these sounds are spelled only one or a few ways.

Learning some onset and rhyme patterns really helps phoneme awareness by showing that just changing the beginning consonant sound can form new words. This can be done before any reading or spelling lessons; it can all be spoken.

## Speech Correction

Young students frequently do not pronounce all the phonemes when speaking. This is sometimes called "baby talk". It is not a serious problem, as some speech sounds are not regularly developed by some children until age 6 or later. However, for good speech, give some practice.

Students who speak a foreign language as a first language often have trouble pronouncing all the phonemes. Some languages do not have all of the phonemes we use in English. Spanish, for example, has no /j/ sound: "general" comes out as "heneral". Some oriental languages like Japanese have no /l/ sound: "luck" comes out like "ruck".

You can give young or foreign students valuable speech correction using selected phonics patterns. Two things you might remember: (1) take off the emotional pressure, never put the student in an embarrassing position, and (2) speech sound production is purely mechanical and habit. You can often see the mechanical problem, like improper tongue placement, by simply placing a mirror in front of the student and letting him watch himself make the sound, then watch you make the sound. The habit formation is developed by giving lots of practice using words with the troubling sound.

## Phonics Rules

A majority of the words in this book follow regular (common) phonics rules such as:

Open Syllable: An open syllable is one that ends in a vowel and the vowel is long.

Closed Syllable: A closed syllable is one that ends in a consonant and the vowel is short.

Final E: In a one syllable word that ends in a silent E preceded by a consonant, the vowel is long (VCe).

Vowel Digraphs: Certain vowel digraphs (2 letter combinations) make the long vowel sound. Example: "ai" as in "paid". Note: the old "double vowel" rule isn't very good because there were too many exceptions like "ou" in "out" or "oo" in "moon".

One way to teach these rules is by some interesting short vowel versus long vowel contrasts such as:

| Final E Rule | Vowel Digraphs | Open & Closed Syllables: |
|---|---|---|
| mad - made | bat - bait | me - met |
| rid - ride | red - reed | go - got |
| rob - robe | got - goat | |
| cub - cube | | |

You will find a lot more examples in this book. An interesting teaching device is a folded flash card in which a letter can be added to the short word by folding over a flap, thereby changing the vowel sound from short to long.

## Make Your Own Worksheets

Teachers often make their own work sheets and often they have very clever ways of doing this. Here are a couple of suggestions:

1. Supply the missing letter to make a real word using these beginning consonant sounds:
   **t, b, h, m, d, gl, cl, etc.**

   | \_\_\_ad | \_\_\_and | \_\_\_ang |
   |---|---|---|
   | \_\_\_ad | \_\_\_and | \_\_\_ang |
   | \_\_\_ad | \_\_\_and | \_\_\_ang |
   | \_\_\_ad | \_\_\_and | \_\_\_ang |

2. Sort these words into similar patterns:
   **bad, gang, sand, bang, mad, etc.**

   | -ad | -nd | -ang |
   |---|---|---|
   | _____ | _____ | _____ |
   | _____ | _____ | _____ |
   | _____ | _____ | _____ |

3. Using the patterns on this page create a funny word for a giraffe, for example, "chang quang".

   Create a funny word for a pink rock _____
   Create a funny word for the space between your toes _____
   Create a funny word for a sick tree _____

# Getting Technical

Perhaps you know the story about the little boy who went into the library and asked the librarian for something about frogs. She gave him several books on frogs, encyclopedia articles on frogs, and a biology text that had pictures of domestic and tropical frogs. Pretty soon she looked over and the little boy was crying. When she asked him what was the trouble, he simply said, "That's more than I want to know about frogs".

Phonics can be like that.

English orthography (our writing and spelling system) can get very complex. Hopefully this book on Phonics Patterns is some sort of sensible compromise between classroom needs and the myriad of details in a phonology, our sound system, course. Like any good reference book it probably has a bit more information (patterns and example words) than you need. But like any good reference book it might present some new information to stretch your knowledge into new vocabulary and new spelling patterns. Good teachers are continually deciding how much information to impart to their students. They need to do the same thing with Phonics Patterns.

English phonology is difficult if you haven't been trained in it (some colleges seem to neglect this for teachers) or if you haven't paid particular attention to it (self teaching). For example, hearing the difference between the Short OO sound in "book" and the Short U sound in "buck". When you have regular and differentiated spelling for the sounds, like our example, it makes it somewhat easier. But how about hearing the same difference when the Short OO Sound is spelled with a U in "full" and the Short U sound is spelled with an O in "come"?

I wrestled with the idea of the Long U sound as is in some older phonics systems. After all, all the other vowels have a long and a short sound, why shouldn't the U have a Long sound (with the Final E Rule), like in the word "fuse"? Three modern dictionaries have told me that there is no such thing as a Long U. A word like "fuse" is really /f/+/y/ +/oo/+/z/. This is, of course, different from a word like "June", which just has the /oo/ sound with no /y/. But, then again, in some quite proper American accents, the /y/ is pronounced in "June". Ah me, see the problem of getting too detailed. So to simplify I tossed all the/oo/ sounds under the Long OO section, whether or not there was a /y/ in front of the /oo/. If you want to teach that there is a Final E Rule for the U, and illustrate it with patterns like those found in "cube", "rude' or "June", help yourself. You'll find them under the Long OO section.

For those scholars who wish to know how these Phonics Patterns were derived, basically I went all the way through two rhyming dictionaries and one dissertation seeking out patterns and example words. I edited out what I judged to be obscure words and small 2 word patterns in which neither word was very common. This took a lot of hours. But when I realized that thousands of teachers have already bought earlier editions of this book and that those thousands of teachers are teaching many thousands more children, it all seemed worth the effort. My basic training was that of an educational psychologist, and one of the jobs of an educational psychologist is to translate good research into usable form for teachers out there on the firing line. I hope I have done that.

E. F.

References
Alee, J.G. (Prof. of English Philology, George Washington Univ.) "Rhyming Dictionary" in Webster's Encyclopedia of Dictionaries. Ottenheimer Publishers, Baltimore,MD, 1983

Stanback, M.L., "Syllable and Rime Patterns for Teaching Reading: Analysis of a Frequency Based Vocabulary of 17,602 Words" Unpublished dissertation, Teachers College, Columbia Univ. 1991.

Webster's Compact Rhyming Dictionary. Merriam-Webster Inc., Springfield, MA 1987.

# Short A Sound

**Dictionary Phonetic Symbol: All /a/**

Phonics: Closed Syllable Rule - When a single vowel is
followed by a consonant, the vowel is short (no final "e").

## -ab

| | |
|---|---|
| cab | blab |
| dab | crab |
| gab | drab |
| jab | flab |
| lab | grab |
| nab | scab |
| tab | slab |
| | stab |

## -ack

| | |
|---|---|
| back | black |
| hack | clack |
| Jack | crack |
| lack | knack |
| Mack | shack |
| pack | slack |
| sack | smack |
| tack | snack |
| | stack |
| | track |
| | whack |

## -act

| |
|---|
| fact |
| pact |
| tact |
| tract |

## -ad

| | | |
|---|---|---|
| bad | lad | Brad |
| cad | mad | Chad |
| dad | pad | clad |
| fad | sad | glad |
| gad | tad | shad |
| had | | |

## -aff

| |
|---|
| gaff |
| chaff |
| quaff |
| staff |

## -aft

| |
|---|
| daft |
| raft |
| waft |
| craft |
| draft |
| graft |
| shaft |

**Crab**

# Short A Sound, cont.

<u>Phonics: Closed Syllable Rule</u> - When a single vowel is
followed by a consonant, the vowel is short (no final "e").

## -ag

| | |
|---|---|
| bag | brag |
| gag | crag |
| hag | drag |
| jag | flag |
| lag | shag |
| nag | slag |
| rag | snag |
| sag | stag |
| tag | swag |
| wag | |

## -am

| | |
|---|---|
| cam | clam |
| dam | cram |
| ham | dram |
| jam | gram |
| Pam | scam |
| ram | scram |
| Sam | sham |
| tam | slam |
| yam | swam |
| | tram |

## -amp

| |
|---|
| camp |
| damp |
| lamp |
| ramp |
| tamp |
| vamp |
| champ |
| clamp |
| cramp |
| scamp |
| stamp |
| tramp |

## -an

| | |
|---|---|
| ban | bran |
| can | clan |
| Dan | flan |
| fan | plan |
| man | scan |
| pan | span |
| ran | than |
| tan | |
| van | |

## -ance

| |
|---|
| dance |
| lance |
| chance |
| France |
| glance |
| prance |
| stance |
| trance |

## -anch

| |
|---|
| ranch |
| blanch |
| branch |
| stanch |

## -and

| |
|---|
| band |
| hand |
| land |
| sand |
| bland |
| brand |
| gland |
| stand |

# Short A Sound, cont.

**Dictionary Phonetic Symbol: All /a/**

<u>Phonics: Closed Syllable Rule</u> - When a single vowel is
followed by a consonant, the vowel is short (no final "e").

## -ang

bang
fang
gang
hang
pang
rang
sang
tang
clang
slang
sprang

## -ank

| | |
|---|---|
| bank | blank |
| dank | clank |
| hank | crank |
| lank | drank |
| rank | flank |
| sank | Frank |
| tank | plank |
| yank | prank |
| | shank |
| | spank |
| | thank |

## -ant

can't
pant
rant
chant
grant
plant
scant
slant

## -ap (cont.)

cap
gap
lap
map
nap
pap
rap
sap
tap
yap

## -ap

(continued)

chap
clap
flap
scrap
slap
snap
strap
trap
wrap

## -ash

| | |
|---|---|
| bash | brash |
| cash | clash |
| dash | flash |
| gash | slash |
| hash | smash |
| lash | stash |
| mash | thrash |
| rash | trash |
| sash | |

## -ask

ask
cask
mask
task
flask

## -asm

chasm
plasm
spasm

**Plant**

# Short A Sound, cont.

**Dictionary Phonetic Symbol: All /a/**

Phonics: Closed Syllable Rule - When a single vowel is
followed by a consonant, the vowel is short (no final "e").

| -asp | -ass | -ast | -at | |
|------|------|------|-----|------|
| gasp | bass | cast | bat | brat |
| hasp | lass | fast | cat | chat |
| rasp | mass | last | fat | drat |
| clasp | pass | mast | gnat | flat |
| | brass | past | hat | scat |
| | class | vast | mat | slat |
| | glass | blast | pat | spat |
| | | | rat | that |
| | | | sat | |
| | | | tat | |
| | | | vat | |

| -atch | -ath | -ax |
|-------|------|-----|
| batch | bath | lax |
| catch | lath | Max |
| hatch | math | tax |
| latch | path | wax |
| match | wrath | flax |
| patch | | |
| scratch | | |
| snatch | | |
| thatch | | |

**Hat**

# Long A Sound

**Dictionary Phonetic Symbol: All /ā/**

<u>Phonics: Final E Rule</u> - A silent "e" at the end of a word following a consonant makes the vowel long.
<u>Phonics: Vowel Digraphs</u> - The following digraphs (2 vowels together) make the long A sound; "ai" and "ay".
(Exceptions marked with an asterisk*)

| -ace | -ade | -age | -aid | -ail (cont.) |
|------|------|------|------|--------------|
| face | bade | cage | laid | bail |
| lace | fade | gage | maid | fail |
| mace | jade | page | paid | Gail |
| pace | made | rage | raid | hail |
| race | wade | sage | braid | jail |
| brace | blade | wage | staid | mail |
| grace | glade | stage | | nail |
| place | grade | | | pail |
| space | shade | | | quail |
| trace | spade | | | rail |
| | trade | | | sail |
| | | | | tail |
| | | | | wail |

| -ail | -ain | | -aint | -aise |
|------|------|------|-------|-------|
| (continued) | lain | brain | faint | raise |
| flail | main | chain | paint | braise |
| frail | pain | drain | saint | chaise |
| snail | rain | grain | taint | praise |
| trail | vain | plain | quaint | |
| | wain | slain | | |
| | | Spain | | |
| | | sprain | | |
| | | stain | | |
| | | strain | | |
| | | train | | |

**Snail**

# Long A Sound, cont.

Phonics: Final E Rule - A silent "e" at the end of a word following a consonant makes the vowel long.
Phonics: Vowel Digraphs - The following digraphs (2 vowels together) make the long A sound; "ai" and "ay".
(Exceptions marked with an asterisk*)

## -ait

bait
gait
wait
strait
trait

## -ake

| | |
|---|---|
| bake | brake |
| cake | drake |
| fake | flake |
| Jake | shake |
| lake | snake |
| make | |
| quake | |
| rake | |
| take | |
| wake | |

## -ale

| | |
|---|---|
| bale | scale |
| dale | shale |
| gale | |
| hale | |
| male | |
| pale | |
| sale | |
| tale | |

## -ame

came
dame
fame
game
lame
name
same
tame
blame
flame
frame
shame

## -ane

bane
cane
Jane
lane
mane
pane
sane
vane
wane
crane
plane

## -ange

mange
range
change
grange
strange

## -ape

cape
gape
nape
rape
tape
drape
grape
scrape
shape

## -ase

base
case
vase
chase

**Grapes**

Phonics Patterns  •  by Edward Fry  •  Laguna Beach Educational Books

17

# Long A Sound, cont.

## Dictionary Phonetic Symbol: All /ā/

Phonics: Final E Rule - A silent "e" at the end of a word following a consonant makes the vowel long.
Phonics: Vowel Digraphs - The following digraphs (2 vowels together) make the long A sound; "ai" and "ay".
(Exceptions marked with an asterisk*)

| -aste | -ate | -ave | -ay | |
|-------|------|------|-----|---|
| baste | date | cave | bay | bray |
| haste | fate | Dave | day | clay |
| paste | gate | gave | gay | cray |
| taste | hate | pave | hay | fray |
| waste | Kate | rave | jay | gray |
| chaste | late | save | lay | play |
| | mate | wave | may | pray |
| | rate | brave | nay | slay |
| | crate | crave | pay | spray |
| | grate | grave | quay | stay |
| | plate | shave | ray | stray |
| | skate | slave | say | sway |
| | state | stave | way | tray |

| -aze | -eak* | -eigh* | -ey* |
|------|-------|--------|------|
| daze | break | neigh | hey |
| faze | steak | weigh | grey |
| gaze | | sleigh | prey |
| haze | | | they |
| maze | | | whey |
| raze | | | |
| blaze | | | |
| craze | | | |
| glaze | | | |
| graze | | | |

**Sleigh**

# Broad A Sound

## Dictionary Phonetic Symbol: All /ä/

Phonics: - When the letter "r" follows the vowel, it is neither long or short.
Letter "r" following "a" makes the broad "a" sound.

| -atch* | -ar | -ard | -arge | -ark |
|--------|-----|------|-------|------|
| watch | bar | bard | barge | bark |
| swatch | car | card | large | dark |
| | far | guard | charge | hark |
| | jar | hard | | lark |
| | mar | lard | | mark |
| | par | yard | | park |
| | tar | shard | | Clark |
| | char | | | shark |
| | scar | | | spark |
| | spar | | | stark |
| | star | | | |

| -arl | -arm | -arn | -arp | -art |
|------|------|------|------|------|
| Carl | farm | barn | carp | cart |
| snarl | harm | darn | harp | dart |
| | charm | yarn | tarp | mart |
| | | | sharp | part |
| | | | | tart |
| | | | | chart |
| | | | | smart |
| | | | | start |

**Harp**

# Short E Sound

**Dictionary Phonetic Symbol: All /e/**

Phonics: Closed Syllable Rule - When a single vowel is followed by a consonant, the vowel is short (no final "e").
Phonics: Vowel Digraphs - "ea" sometimes makes the short "e" sound, but not usually.
(Exceptions marked with an asterisk*)

| -air* | -are* | | -ead | -ear |
|---|---|---|---|---|
| air | bare | blare | dead | bear |
| fair | care | flare | head | pear |
| hair | dare | glare | lead | wear |
| lair | fare | scare | read | swear |
| pair | hare | share | bread | |
| chair | mare | snare | dread | |
| flair | pare | spare | spread | |
| stair | rare | square | thread | |
| | ware | stare | tread | |

| -ealth | -eath | -eck | -ed | |
|---|---|---|---|---|
| health | death | deck | bed | bled |
| wealth | breath | heck | fed | bred |
| stealth | | neck | led | fled |
| | | peck | Ned | Fred |
| | | check | red | shed |
| | | fleck | Ted | shred |
| | | speck | wed | sled |
| | | wreck | | sped |

**Bed**

# Short E Sound, cont.

**Dictionary Phonetic Symbol: All /e/**

<u>Phonics: Closed Syllable Rule</u> - When a single vowel is followed by a consonant, the vowel is short (no final "e").
<u>Phonics: Vowel Digraphs</u> - "ea" sometimes makes the short "e" sound, but not usually.
(Exceptions marked with an asterisk*)

| **-edge** | **-eft** | **-eg** | **-eld** | **-elf** |
|---|---|---|---|---|
| hedge | deft | beg | held | self |
| ledge | heft | keg | meld | shelf |
| wedge | left | leg | weld | |
| dredge | cleft | meg | | |
| pledge | theft | peg | | |
| sledge | | | | |

**Gem**

| **-ell** | | **-elp** | **-elt** | **-em** |
|---|---|---|---|---|
| bell | dwell | help | belt | gem |
| cell | quell | kelp | felt | hem |
| dell | shell | yelp | knelt | stem |
| fell | smell | | melt | them |
| hell | spell | | pelt | |
| jell | swell | | welt | |
| knell | | | dwelt | |
| Nell | | | smelt | |
| sell | | | | |
| tell | | | | |
| well | | | | |
| yell | | | | |

# Short E Sound, cont.

## Dictionary Phonetic Symbol: All /e/

Phonics: Closed Syllable Rule - When a single vowel is followed by a consonant, the vowel is short (no final "e").
Phonics: Vowel Digraphs - "ea" sometimes makes the short "e" sound, but not usually.
(Exceptions marked with an asterisk*)

| -en | -ence | -ench | -end | -ength |
|-----|-------|-------|------|--------|
| Ben | fence | bench | bend | trend |
| den | hence | wench | end | length |
| hen | pence | clench | fend | strength |
| Ken | whence | drench | lend | |
| men | | French | mend | |
| pen | | quench | rend | |
| ten | | stench | send | |
| yen | | trench | tend | |
| glen | | wrench | vend | |
| then | | | wend | |
| when | | | blend | |
| wren | | | spend | |

| -ense | -ent | -ep | -ept | -esh |
|-------|------|-----|------|------|
| dense | bent | spent | kept | mesh |
| sense | cent | pep | wept | flesh |
| tense | dent | rep | crept | fresh |
| | gent | prep | slept | |
| | Kent | step | swept | |
| | lent | | | |
| | rent | | | |
| | sent | | | |
| | tent | | | |
| | vent | | | |
| | went | | | |
| | scent | | | |

**Wrench**

# Short E Sound, cont.

**Dictionary Phonetic Symbol: All /e/**

Phonics: Closed Syllable Rule - When a single vowel is followed by a consonant, the vowel is short (no final "e").
Phonics: Vowel Digraphs - "ea" sometimes makes the short "e" sound, but not usually.
(Exceptions marked with an asterisk*)

| -ess | -est | | -et | |
|------|------|------|-----|------|
| Bess | best | blest | bet | Chet |
| guess | quest | chest | get | fret |
| less | jest | crest | jet | whet |
| mess | lest | quest | let | |
| bless | nest | wrest | met | |
| chess | pest | | net | |
| dress | rest | | pet | |
| press | test | | set | |
| stress | vest | | wet | |
| tress | west | | yet | |
| | zest | | | |

| -etch | -ex | -ext |
|-------|-----|------|
| fetch | hex | next |
| retch | sex | text |
| sketch | vex | |
| wretch | flex | |

**Jet**

# √Long E Sound

**Dictionary Phonetic Symbol: All /ē/**

Phonics: Open Syllable Rule - When the syllable ends in a vowel, it is long.
Phonics: Vowel Digraphs - "ea", "ee" and "ie" make the long "e" sound.
(Exceptions marked with an asterisk*)

| -e | -ea | -each | -ead | -eak |
|----|-----|-------|------|------|
| be | pea | beach | bead | beak |
| he | sea | leach | lead | leak |
| me | tea | peach | read | peak |
| we | flea | reach | knead | teak |
| she | plea | teach | plead | weak |
| | | bleach | | bleak |
| | | breach | | creak |
| | | preach | | freak |
| | | | | sneak |
| | | | | speak |
| | | | | squeak |
| | | | | streak |
| | | | | tweak |

**Peach**

| -eal | -eam | -ean | -eap | -ear |
|------|------|------|------|------|
| deal | beam | bean | heap | dear |
| heal | ream | dean | leap | fear |
| meal | seam | Jean | reap | gear |
| peal | cream | lean | cheap | hear |
| real | dream | mean | | near |
| seal | gleam | wean | | rear |
| teal | scream | clean | | sear |
| veal | steam | glean | | tear |
| zeal | stream | | | year |
| squeal | team | | | clear |
| steal | | | | shear |
| | | | | smear |
| | | | | spear |

# Long E Sound, cont.

**Dictionary Phonetic Symbol: All /ē/**

<u>Phonics: Open Syllable Rule</u> - When the syllable ends in a vowel, it is long.
<u>Phonics: Vowel Digraphs</u> - "ea", "ee" and "ie" make the long "e" sound.
(Exceptions marked with an asterisk*)

| -ease | -east | -eat | -eath | -eave |
|-------|-------|------|-------|-------|
| cease | beast | beat | heath | heave |
| lease | feast | feat | sheath | leave |
| crease | least | heat | wreath | weave |
| grease | yeast | meat | | cleave |
| | | neat | | sheave |
| | | peat | | |
| | | seat | | |
| | | bleat | | |
| | | cheat | | |
| | | cleat | | |
| | | pleat | | |

**Meat**

| -ee | -eech | -eed | -eef | -eek |
|-----|-------|------|------|------|
| bee | beech | deed | beef | leek |
| fee | leech | feed | reef | meek |
| knee | breech | heed | | peek |
| lee | screech | kneed | | reek |
| see | speech | need | | seek |
| tee | | reed | | week |
| wee | | seed | | cheek |
| flee | | weed | | creek |
| free | | bleed | | Greek |
| glee | | breed | | sleek |
| three | | creed | | |
| spree | | freed | | |
| tree | | greed | | |

# Long E Sound, cont.
## Dictionary Phonetic Symbol: All /ē/
Phonics: Open Syllable Rule - When the syllable ends in a vowel, it is long.
Phonics: Vowel Digraphs - "ea", "ee" and "ie" make the long "e" sound.
(Exceptions marked with an asterisk*)

| -eel | -eem | -een | -eep | -eer |
|------|------|------|------|------|
| feel | deem | keen | beep | beer |
| heel | seem | queen | deep | deer |
| keel | teem | seen | jeep | jeer |
| kneel | | teen | keep | leer |
| peel | | green | peep | peer |
| reel | | preen | seep | queer |
| creel | | screen | weep | seer |
| steel | | sheen | cheep | sneer |
| wheel | | | creep | steer |
| | | | sleep | |
| | | | steep | |
| | | | sweep | |

| -eet | -eeze* | -iece* | -ief | -ield |
|------|--------|--------|------|-------|
| beet | breeze | niece | brief | field |
| feet | freeze | piece | chief | yield |
| meet | sneeze | | grief | shield |
| fleet | squeeze | | thief | |
| greet | tweeze | | | |
| sheet | wheeze | | | |
| skeet | | | | |
| sleet | | | | |
| street | | | | |
| sweet | | | | |
| tweet | | | | |

**Deer**

# Short I Sound

**Dictionary Phonetic Symbol: All /i/**

<u>Phonics: Closed Syllable Rule</u> - When a single vowel is followed by a consonant, the vowel is short (no final "e").
(Exceptions marked with an asterisk*)

| -ib | -ick | | -id | -idge |
|-----|------|------|-----|-------|
| bib | Dick | brick | bid | ridge |
| fib | hick | chick | did | bridge |
| jib | kick | click | hid | |
| rib | lick | flick | kid | |
| crib | Nick | slick | lid | |
| glib | pick | stick | mid | |
| | quick | thick | quid | |
| | Rick | trick | rid | |
| | sick | | grid | |
| | tick | | skid | |
| | wick | | slid | |

| -iff | -ift | -ig | | -ilk |
|------|------|-----|------|------|
| miff | gift | big | pig | bilk |
| tiff | lift | dig | rig | milk |
| cliff | rift | fig | wig | silk |
| skiff | sift | gig | brig | |
| sniff | drift | jig | sprig | |
| stiff | shift | | swig | |
| whiff | swift | | twig | |
| | thrift | | | |

**Milk**

# Short I Sound, cont.
## Dictionary Phonetic Symbol: All /i/

Phonics: Closed Syllable Rule - When a single vowel is followed by a consonant, the vowel is short (no final "e").
(Exceptions marked with an asterisk*)

## -ill

| | |
|---|---|
| bill | till |
| dill | will |
| fill | chill |
| gill | drill |
| hill | frill |
| ill | grill |
| Jill | skill |
| kill | spill |
| mill | still |
| pill | swill |
| quill | thrill |
| rill | trill |
| sill | twill |

## -ilt

| |
|---|
| gilt |
| jilt |
| hilt |
| kilt |
| tilt |
| wilt |
| quilt |
| stilt |

## -im

| | |
|---|---|
| dim | brim |
| him | grim |
| Jim | prim |
| Kim | slim |
| rim | swim |
| Tim | trim |
| vim | whim |

## -imp

| |
|---|
| limp |
| chimp |
| crimp |
| primp |
| skimp |
| blimp |

## -in

| | |
|---|---|
| bin | chin |
| din | grin |
| fin | shin |
| gin | skin |
| kin | spin |
| pin | thin |
| sin | twin |
| tin | |
| win | |

## -ince

| |
|---|
| mince |
| since |
| wince |
| prince |

## -inch

| |
|---|
| inch |
| cinch |
| finch |
| pinch |
| winch |
| Grinch |
| clinch |
| flinch |

<u>Phonics: Closed Syllable Rule</u> - When a single vowel is followed by a consonant, the vowel is short (no final "e").
(Exceptions marked with an asterisk*)

## -ing

| | |
|---|---|
| bing | bring |
| ding | cling |
| king | fling |
| ping | sling |
| ring | spring |
| sing | sting |
| wing | string |
| zing | swing |
| | thing |
| | wring |

## -inge

binge
hinge
singe
tinge
cringe
fringe
twinge

## -ink

| | |
|---|---|
| kink | blink |
| link | brink |
| mink | chink |
| pink | clink |
| rink | drink |
| sink | shrink |
| wink | slink |
| | stink |
| | think |

## -int

hint
lint
mint
tint
glint
print
splint
sprint
squint

## -ip

| | |
|---|---|
| dip | blip |
| hip | chip |
| lip | clip |
| nip | drip |
| quip | flip |
| rip | grip |
| sip | ship |
| tip | skip |
| zip | slip |
| | snip |
| | strip |
| | trip |
| | whip |

## -is

is
his

## -ish

dish
fish
wish
swish

**King**

# Short I Sound, cont.
## Dictionary Phonetic Symbol: All /i/

Phonics: Closed Syllable Rule - When a single vowel is followed by a consonant, the vowel is short (no final "e").
(Exceptions marked with an asterisk*)

| -isk | -isp | -iss | -ist |
|---|---|---|---|
| disk | lisp | hiss | fist |
| risk | wisp | kiss | list |
| brisk | crisp | miss | mist |
| frisk | | bliss | wrist |
| whisk | | Swiss | grist |
| | | | twist |

**Witch**

| -it | | -itch | -ive* | -ix |
|---|---|---|---|---|
| bit | flit | ditch | give | fix |
| fit | grit | hitch | live | mix |
| hit | skit | pitch | | six |
| kit | slit | witch | | |
| knit | spit | switch | | |
| lit | split | | | |
| pit | twit | | | |
| quit | | | | |
| sit | | | | |
| wit | | | | |

**Six**

Phonics Patterns • by Edward Fry • Laguna Beach Educational Books

# ✓Long I Sound

**Dictionary Phonetic Symbol: All /ī/**

<u>Phonics: Final E Rule</u> - A silent "e" at the end of a word following a consonant makes the vowel long.
<u>Phonics: Vowel Digraphs</u> - "ie" makes the long "i" sound.
(Exceptions marked with an asterisk*)

| -ibe | -ice | -ide | -ie | -ied |
|------|------|------|-----|------|
| jibe | dice | bide | die | |
| bribe | lice | hide | fie | died |
| scribe | mice | ride | lie | lied |
| tribe | nice | side | pie | cried |
| | rice | tide | tie | dried |
| | vice | wide | vie | fried |
| | price | bride | | spied |
| | slice | chide | | tried |
| | splice | glide | | |
| | thrice | pride | | |
| | twice | slide | | |
| | | snide | | |
| | | stride | | |

**Tie**

| -ier | -ies | -ife | -igh* | -ight* |
|------|------|------|-------|--------|
| brier | dies | fife | high | fight |
| crier | lies | knife | sigh | knight |
| drier | pies | life | nigh | light |
| flier | ties | rife | thigh | might |
| | cries | wife | | night |
| | dries | strife | | right |
| | flies | | | sight |
| | spies | | | tight |

(continued next page)

# Long I Sound, cont.
## Dictionary Phonetic Symbol: All /ī/

Phonics: Final E Rule - A silent "e" at the end of a word following a consonant makes the vowel long.
Phonics: Vowel Digraphs - "ie" makes the long "i" sound.
(Exceptions marked with an asterisk*)

| -ight* | -ike | -ild* | -ile | -ime |
|--------|------|-------|------|------|
| (continued) | bike | mild | bile | dime |
| blight | dike | wild | file | lime |
| bright | hike | child | mile | mime |
| flight | like | | Nile | time |
| fright | Mike | | pile | chime |
| plight | pike | | tile | clime |
| slight | spike | | vile | crime |
| | strike | | smile | grime |
| | | | stile | prime |
| | | | while | slime |

**Bike**

| -ind* | -ine | | -ipe |
|-------|------|---|------|
| bind | dine | tine | pipe |
| find | fine | vine | ripe |
| hind | line | wine | wipe |
| kind | mine | brine | gripe |
| mind | nine | shine | snipe |
| wind | pine | shrine | stripe |
| blind | | spine | swipe |
| grind | | swine | |
| | | whine | |

# Long I Sound, cont.

## Dictionary Phonetic Symbol: All /ī/

Phonics: Final E Rule - A silent "e" at the end of a word following a consonant makes the vowel long.
Phonics: Vowel Digraphs - "ie" makes the long "i" sound.
(Exceptions marked with an asterisk*)

| -ire | -ise | -ite | -ive | -ize |
|------|------|------|------|------|
| fire | guise | bite | dive | size |
| hire | rise | kite | five | prize |
| tire | wise | mite | hive | |
| wire | | quite | jive | |
| spire | | rite | live | |
| | | site | chive | |
| | | white | drive | |

**Kite**

| -uy* | -y* | | -ye* |
|------|-----|------|------|
| buy | by | spy | aye |
| guy | my | spry | bye |
| | cry | sty | dye |
| | dry | thy | eye |
| | fly | try | lye |
| | fry | why | rye |
| | ply | | |
| | pry | | |
| | shy | | |
| | sky | | |
| | sly | | |

**Fire**

# Short O Sound

**Dictionary Phonetic Symbol:  Thorndike & Random /o/, Webster /ä/**

<u>Phonics: Closed Syllable Rule</u> - When a single vowel is followed by a consonant, the vowel is short (no final "e").
(Exceptions marked with an asterisk*)

## -ob

| | |
|---|---|
| Bob | blob |
| cob | glob |
| fob | slob |
| gob | snob |
| job | throb |
| knob | |
| lob | |
| mob | |
| rob | |
| sob | |

## -ock

| | |
|---|---|
| dock | block |
| hock | clock |
| knock | crock |
| lock | flock |
| mock | frock |
| rock | shock |
| sock | smock |
| tock | |

## -od

| |
|---|
| cod |
| God |
| mod |
| nod |
| pod |
| rod |
| sod |
| clod |
| plod |
| prod |
| shod |
| trod |

## -oft

| |
|---|
| loft |
| soft |

## -og

| |
|---|
| bog |
| cog |
| dog |
| fog |
| hog |
| jog |
| log |
| tog |
| clog |
| flog |
| frog |
| grog |

## -oll

| |
|---|
| doll |
| loll |
| moll |

## -omp

| |
|---|
| pomp |
| romp |
| chomp |
| stomp |

## -ond

| |
|---|
| bond |
| fond |
| pond |
| blond |
| frond |

**Doll**

# Short O Sound, cont.

**Dictionary Phonetic Symbol: Thorndike & Random /o/, Webster /ä/**

<u>Phonics: Closed Syllable Rule</u> - When a single vowel is followed by a consonant, the vowel is short (no final "e").
(Exceptions marked with an asterisk*)

## -op

| | |
|---|---|
| bop | chop |
| cop | crop |
| hop | drop |
| mop | flop |
| pop | plop |
| sop | prop |
| top | shop |
| | slop |
| | stop |

## -ot

| | |
|---|---|
| cot | blot |
| dot | clot |
| got | plot |
| hot | shot |
| jot | slot |
| knot | spot |
| lot | trot |
| not | |
| pot | |
| rot | |
| tot | |

## -otch

botch
notch
blotch
crotch
Scotch

## -ough*

cough
trough

## -ox

box
fox
lox
pox

**Stop**

ox

# Long O Sound

**Dictionary Phonetic Symbol: All /ō/**

Phonics: Open Syllable Rule - When the syllable ends in a vowel, it is long.
Phonics: Vowel Digraphs - "oa" makes the long "o" sound and "ow" sometimes makes the long "o" sound.
Phonics: Final E Rule - A silent "e" at the end of a word following a consonant makes the vowel long.
(Exceptions marked with an asterisk*)

| -o | -oach | -oad | -oak | -oal |
|---|---|---|---|---|
| go | coach | goad | soak | coal |
| no | poach | load | cloak | foal |
| so | roach | road | croak | goal |
| pro | broach | toad | | shoal |

**Toad**

| -oam | -oan | -oast | -oat | -obe |
|---|---|---|---|---|
| foam | Joan | boast | oat | lobe |
| loam | loan | coast | boat | robe |
| roam | moan | roast | coat | globe |
| | groan | toast | goat | probe |
| | | | moat | |
| | | | bloat | |
| | | | float | |
| | | | gloat | |
| | | | throat | |

**Dictionary Phonetic Symbol: All /ō/**

Phonics: Open Syllable Rule - When the syllable ends in a vowel, it is long.
Phonics: Vowel Digraphs - "oa" makes the long "o" sound and "ow" sometimes makes the long "o" sound.
Phonics: Final E Rule - A silent "e" at the end of a word following a consonant makes the vowel long.
(Exceptions marked with an asterisk*)

| -ode | -oe* | -ogue | -oke | -old* |
|------|------|-------|------|-------|
| code | doe | rogue | coke | bold |
| lode | foe | vogue | joke | cold |
| mode | hoe | brogue | poke | fold |
| node | Joe | | woke | gold |
| rode | roe | | yoke | hold |
| strode | toe | | broke | mold |
| | woe | | choke | old |
| | | | smoke | sold |
| | | | spoke | told |
| | | | stoke | scold |
| | | | stroke | |

**Globe**

| -ole | -oll | -olt | -ome | -one |
|------|------|------|------|------|
| dole | poll | bolt | dome | bone |
| hole | roll | colt | home | cone |
| mole | toll | jolt | Nome | hone |
| pole | droll | molt | Rome | lone |
| role | knoll | volt | tome | tone |
| stole | scroll | | gnome | zone |
| whole | stroll | | chrome | clone |
| | | | | crone |
| | | | | drone |
| | | | | phone |
| | | | | prone |
| | | | | shone |
| | | | | stone |

# Long O Sound, cont.

**Dictionary Phonetic Symbol: All /ō/**

<u>Phonics: Open Syllable Rule</u> - When the syllable ends in a vowel, it is long.
<u>Phonics: Vowel Digraphs</u> - "oa" makes the long "o" sound and "ow" sometimes makes the long "o" sound.
<u>Phonics: Final E Rule</u> - A silent "e" at the end of a word following a consonant makes the vowel long.
(Exceptions marked with an asterisk*)

| **-ont** | **-ope** | **-ose** | **-ost** | **-ote** |
|---|---|---|---|---|
| don't | cope | hose | host | note |
| won't | dope | nose | most | quote |
|  | hope | pose | post | rote |
|  | lope | rose | ghost | vote |
|  | mope | chose |  | wrote |
|  | nope | close |  |  |
|  | pope | prose |  |  |
|  | rope | those |  |  |
|  | scope |  |  |  |
|  | slope |  |  |  |

**Rose**

| **-ove** | **-ow** |  | **-own** |
|---|---|---|---|
| cove | bow | blow | known |
| wove | know | crow | mown |
| clove | low | flow | sown |
| drove | mow | glow | blown |
| grove | row | grow | flown |
| stove | sow | show | grown |
| trove | tow | slow | shown |
|  |  | snow |  |
|  |  | stow |  |

# Short OO Sound

**Dictionary Phonetic Symbol: Thorndike & Webster /ủ/, Random /ŏŏ/**

<u>Phonics: Vowel Digraphs</u> - "oo" sometimes makes the short "oo" sound.
(Exceptions marked with an asterisk*)

| -ood | -ook | -oor | -oot | -ould* |
|------|------|------|------|--------|
| good | book | boor | foot | could |
| hood | cook | poor | soot | would |
| wood | hook | moor | | should |
| stood | look | spoor | | |
| | nook | | | |
| | took | | | |
| | brook | | | |
| | crook | | | |
| | shook | | | |

| -ull* | -ush* |
|-------|-------|
| bull | bush |
| full | push |
| pull | |

**Book**

# Long OO Sound

**Dictionary Phonetic Symbol: Thorndike & Webster / ü /, Random / o͞o /**

<u>Phonics: Vowel Digraphs</u> - "oo" sometimes makes the long "oo" sound.
(Exceptions marked with an asterisk*)  See discussion of long "u" on page 11.

| -ew* | | -o* | -oo | -ood |
|---|---|---|---|---|
| dew | blew | do | boo | shoo |
| few | brew | to | coo | food |
| hew | chew | who | goo | mood |
| Jew | crew | | moo | brood |
| knew | drew | | too | |
| new | flew | | woo | |
| pew | grew | | zoo | |
| | screw | | | |
| | skew | | | |
| | slew | | | |
| | stew | | | |
| | threw | | | |

**Broom**

| -oof | -ool | -oom | -oon | -oop |
|---|---|---|---|---|
| goof | cool | boom | boon | coop |
| roof | fool | doom | coon | hoop |
| proof | pool | loom | loon | loop |
| spoof | tool | room | moon | droop |
| | drool | zoom | noon | scoop |
| | school | bloom | soon | sloop |
| | spool | broom | croon | snoop |
| | stool | gloom | spoon | stoop |
| | | groom | swoon | swoop |
| | | | | troop |

# Long OO Sound, cont.

**Dictionary Phonetic Symbol: Thorndike & Webster / ü /, Random / o͞o /**

Phonics: Vowel Digraphs - "oo" sometimes makes the long "oo" sound.
(Exceptions marked with an asterisk*) See discussion of long "u" on page 11.

| -oose | -oot | -ooth | -ose | -ooze* |
|-------|------|-------|------|--------|
| goose | boot | booth | lose | booze |
| loose | hoot | tooth | whose | ooze |
| moose | loot | | | snooze |
| noose | moot | | | soup |
| | root | | | croup |
| | toot | | | group |
| | scoot | | | |
| | shoot | | | |

**Boot**

| -oup* | -ube | -uce | -ude | -ue |
|-------|------|------|------|-----|
| soup | cube | spruce | dude | due |
| croup | lube | truce | nude | hue |
| group | rube | | rude | Sue |
| | tube | | crude | blue |
| | | | prude | clue |
| | | | | flue |
| | | | | glue |
| | | | | true |

**Glue**

Phonics Patterns • by Edward Fry • Laguna Beach Educational Books

# Long OO Sound, cont.
## Dictionary Phonetic Symbol: Thorndike & Webster /ü/, Random /o͞o/

Phonics: Vowel Digraphs - "oo" sometimes makes the long "oo" sound.
(Exceptions marked with an asterisk*) See discussion of long "u" on page 11.

| -uke | -ule | -ume | -une | -ure |
|------|------|------|------|------|
| duke | mule | fume | dune | cure |
| nuke | rule | flume | June | lure |
| puke | yule | plume | tune | pure |
| fluke | | spume | prune | sure |

| -use | -ute | -uth |
|------|------|------|
| fuse | cute | Ruth |
| muse | jute | truth |
| | lute | |
| | mute | |
| | brute | |
| | chute | |
| | flute | |

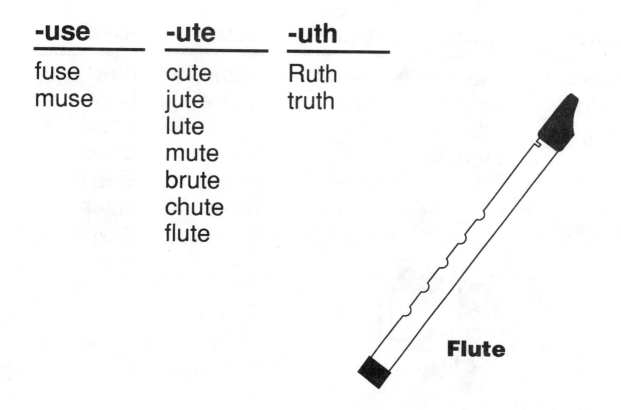

**Flute**

Phonics Patterns    •    by Edward Fry    •    Laguna Beach Educational Books

# Broad O Sound

**Dictionary Phonetic Symbol: Thorndike & Random /ô/, Webster /ȯ/**

Phonics - The broad "o" sound is spelled a number of ways.
Some of the most common are "al", "aw" and "or".

| -alf | -all | -alk | -alt | -aught |
|------|------|------|------|--------|
| calf | ball | balk | halt | caught |
| half | call | talk | malt | naught |
|      | fall | walk | salt | taught |
|      | gall | chalk |     | fraught |
|      | hall | stalk |     |        |
|      | mall |      |      |        |
|      | pall |      |      |        |
|      | tall |      |      |        |
|      | wall |      |      |        |
|      | small |     |      |        |
|      | squall |    |      |        |
|      | stall |     |      |        |

**Malt**

| -ault | -aunch | -aunt | -aw | -awl |
|-------|--------|-------|-----|------|
| fault | haunch | daunt | caw | bawl |
| vault | launch | gaunt | gnaw | brawl |
|       | paunch | haunt | jaw | crawl |
|       | staunch | jaunt | law | drawl |
|       |        | taunt | paw | shawl |
|       |        | flaunt | raw | scrawl |
|       |        |       | saw | trawl |
|       |        |       | claw |     |
|       |        |       | draw |     |
|       |        |       | flaw |     |
|       |        |       | slaw |     |
|       |        |       | squaw |    |
|       |        |       | straw |    |

# Broad O Sound, cont.

## Dictionary Phonetic Symbol: Thorndike & Random /ô/, Webster /ȯ/

Phonics - The broad "o" sound is spelled a number of ways.
Some of the most common are "al", "aw" and "or".

| -awn | -oar | -ong | -oor | -orch |
|------|------|------|------|-------|
| dawn | boar | bong | door | porch |
| fawn | roar | dong | floor | torch |
| lawn | soar | gong | | scorch |
| pawn | | long | | |
| yawn | | song | | |
| brawn | | tong | | |
| drawn | | prong | | |
| prawn | | strong | | |
| | | thong | | |
| | | throng | | |
| | | wrong | | |

**Door**

| -ord | -ore | | -ork | -orm |
|------|------|------|------|------|
| cord | bore | chore | cork | dorm |
| ford | core | score | fork | form |
| lord | fore | shore | pork | norm |
| chord | gore | snore | York | storm |
| sword | more | spore | stork | |
| | pore | store | | |
| | sore | swore | | |
| | tore | | | |
| | wore | | | |

**Fork**

# Broad O Sound, cont.

**Dictionary Phonetic Symbol: Thorndike & Random /ô/, Webster /ȯ/**

<u>Phonics</u> - The broad "o" sound is spelled a number of ways.
Some of the most common are "al", "aw" and "or".

| -orn | -ort | -oss | -ost | -oth |
|------|------|------|------|------|
| born | fort | boss | cost | moth |
| corn | Mort | loss | lost | broth |
| horn | port | moss | frost | cloth |
| morn | sort | toss | | froth |
| torn | short | cross | | sloth |
| worn | snort | floss | | |
| scorn | sport | gloss | | |
| shorn | | | | |
| sworn | | | | |
| thorn | | | | |

| -ought | -our |
|--------|------|
| bought | four |
| fought | pour |
| ought | |
| sought | |
| brought | |
| thought | |

**Sport**

# OI Sound

**Dictionary Phonetic Symbol: Thorndike & Random /oi/, Webster /ȯi/**

<u>Phonics: Vowel Digraphs</u> - "oi" and "oy" make the same sound.

| **-oice** | **-oil** | **-oin** | **-oint** | **-oise** |
|-----------|----------|----------|-----------|-----------|
| joice | oil | coin | joint | noise |
| voice | boil | join | point | poise |
|  | coil | loin |  |  |
|  | foil | groin |  |  |
|  | soil |  |  |  |
|  | toil |  |  |  |
|  | spoil |  |  |  |
|  | broil |  |  |  |

**Coin**

| **-oist** | **-oy** |
|-----------|---------|
| foist | boy |
| hoist | coy |
| joist | joy |
| moist | Roy |
|  | soy |
|  | toy |
|  | ploy |

# OU Sound

**Dictionary Phonetic Symbol: Thorndike & Random /ou/, Webster /aŭ/**

Phonics: Vowel Digraphs - "ou" and "ow" make the same sound.
Note "ow" also sometimes makes the long "o" sound.

| -ouch | -oud | -ounce | -ound | -ount |
|-------|------|--------|-------|-------|
| couch | loud | ounce | bound | count |
| pouch | cloud | bounce | found | mount |
| vouch | proud | pounce | hound | |
| crouch | | flounce | mound | |
| grouch | | trounce | pound | |
| slouch | | | round | |
| | | | sound | |
| | | | wound | |
| | | | ground | |

**Cloud**

| -our | -ouse | -out | | -outh |
|------|-------|------|------|-------|
| our | douse | out | clout | mouth |
| hour | house | bout | flout | south |
| sour | louse | gout | grout | |
| flour | mouse | lout | scout | |
| scour | rouse | pout | shout | |
| | souse | rout | snout | |
| | blouse | tout | spout | |
| | grouse | | sprout | |
| | spouse | | stout | |
| | | | trout | |

**Dictionary Phonetic Symbol: Thorndike & Random /ou/, Webster /aù/**

Phonics: Vowel Digraphs - "ou" and "ow" make the same sound.
Note "ow" also sometimes makes the long "o" sound.

| -ow | -owl | -own | -owse |
|-----|------|------|-------|
| bow | fowl | down | dowse |
| cow | howl | gown | browse |
| how | jowl | town | drowse |
| now | growl | brown | |
| row | prowl | clown | |
| sow | scowl | crown | |
| vow | | drown | |
| brow | | frown | |
| chow | | | |
| plow | | | |
| prow | | | |

**Clown**

Phonics Patterns  •  by Edward Fry  •  Laguna Beach Educational Books

# Short U Sound

**Dictionary Phonetic Symbol: Thorndike & Random /u/, Webster /ə/**

Phonics: Closed Syllable Rule - When a single vowel is followed by a consonant, the vowel is short (no final "e").
(Exceptions marked with an asterisk*)

| -ome* | -on* | -one* | -ough* | -ove* |
|-------|------|-------|--------|-------|
| come | son | done | rough | dove |
| some | ton | none | tough | love |
| | won | | slough | glove |
| | | | | shove |

**Truck**

| -ub | | -uch | -uck | |
|-----|-----|------|------|------|
| cub | club | much | buck | Chuck |
| dub | drub | such | duck | cluck |
| hub | flub | | luck | pluck |
| nub | grub | | muck | shuck |
| pub | scrub | | puck | stuck |
| rub | shrub | | suck | struck |
| sub | snub | | tuck | truck |
| tub | stub | | | |

# Short U Sound, cont.

**Dictionary Phonetic Symbol: Thorndike & Random /u/, Webster /∂/**

<u>Phonics: Closed Syllable Rule</u> - When a single vowel is followed by a consonant, the vowel is short (no final "e").
(Exceptions marked with an asterisk*)

| -ud | -udge* | -uff | -ug | |
|-----|--------|------|-----|-----|
| bud | budge | buff | bug | chug |
| cud | fudge | cuff | dug | drug |
| dud | judge | huff | hug | plug |
| mud | nudge | muff | jug | shrug |
| crud | drudge | puff | lug | slug |
| spud | grudge | ruff | mug | smug |
| stud | sludge | bluff | pug | snug |
| thud | smudge | fluff | rug | thug |
| | trudge | gruff | tug | |
| | | scuff | | |
| | | sluff | | |
| | | snuff | | |
| | | stuff | | |

| -ulk | -ull | -um | | -umb |
|------|------|-----|-----|------|
| bulk | cull | bum | chum | dumb |
| hulk | dull | gum | drum | numb |
| sulk | gull | hum | glum | crumb |
| | hull | mum | plum | plumb |
| | lull | rum | scum | thumb |
| | mull | sum | slum | |
| | skull | | slum | |
| | | | strum | |
| | | | swum | |

**Bug**

# Short U Sound, cont.

**Dictionary Phonetic Symbol: Thorndike & Random /u/, Webster /∂/**

Phonics: Closed Syllable Rule - When a single vowel is followed by a consonant, the vowel is short (no final "e").
(Exceptions marked with an asterisk*)

## -ump

| | |
|---|---|
| bump | chump |
| dump | clump |
| hump | frump |
| jump | grump |
| lump | plump |
| pump | slump |
| rump | stump |
| | thump |
| | trump |

## -un

bun
fun
gun
nun
pun
run
sun
shun
spun

## -unch

hunch
lunch
munch
punch
brunch
crunch
scrunch

## -ung

dung
hung
lung
rung
sung
clung
flung
slung
sprung
stung
strung
swung
wrung

## -unk

| | |
|---|---|
| bunk | chunk |
| dunk | drunk |
| funk | flunk |
| hunk | plunk |
| junk | shrunk |
| punk | skunk |
| sunk | slunk |
| | spunk |
| | stunk |
| | trunk |

## -unt

bunt
hunt
punt
runt
blunt
grunt
shunt
stunt

## -up

cup
pup
sup

## -us

bus
pus
plus
thus

**Cup**

# Short U Sound, cont.

**Dictionary Phonetic Symbol: Thorndike & Random /u/, Webster /ə/**

Phonics: Closed Syllable Rule - When a single vowel is followed by a consonant, the vowel is short (no final "e"). (Exceptions marked with an asterisk*)

| -ush | -usk | -uss | -ust | -ut |
|------|------|------|------|-----|
| gush | dusk | buss | bust | but |
| hush | husk | fuss | dust | cut |
| lush | tusk | muss | gust | gut |
| mush |      | truss | just | hut |
| rush |      |      | lust | jut |
| blush |      |      | must | nut |
| brush |      |      | rust | rut |
| crush |      |      | crust | Tut |
| flush |      |      | thrust | glut |
| plush |      |      | trust | shut |
| slush |      |      |      | smut |
| thrush |     |      |      | strut |

| -utch | -utt |
|-------|------|
| Dutch | butt |
| hutch | mutt |
| clutch | putt |
| crutch |      |

**Crust**

# UR Sound

**Dictionary Phonetic Symbol: Thorndike /ėr/, Webster /ər/, Random /ûr/**

Phonics: Vowel Digraphs - "er", "ir" and "ur" make the same sound.
(Exceptions marked with an asterisk*)

| -earn* | -erb | -erge | -erk | -erm |
|--------|------|-------|------|------|
| learn | herb | merge | jerk | berm |
| yearn | Serb | serge | clerk | germ |
| | verb | verge | | term |
| | | | | sperm |

**Bird**

| -ern | -erve | -ir | -ird | -irk |
|------|-------|-----|------|------|
| fern | nerve | fir | bird | quirk |
| tern | serve | sir | gird | shirk |
| stern | swerve | stir | third | smirk |
| | | whir | | |

# UR Sound, cont.

**Dictionary Phonetic Symbol: Thorndike /ėr/, Webster /∂r/, Random /ûr/**

Phonics: Vowel Digraphs - "er", "ir" and "ur" make the same sound.
(Exceptions marked with an asterisk*)

| -irl | -irst | -irt | -irth | -ur |
|------|-------|------|-------|-----|
| girl | first | dirt | birth | cur |
| swirl | thirst | flirt | firth | fur |
| twirl | | shirt | girth | blur |
| whirl | | skirt | | slur |
| | | squirt | | |

| -urb | -urge | -urk | -url | -urn |
|------|-------|------|------|------|
| curb | urge | lurk | burl | burn |
| blurb | purge | murk | curl | turn |
| | | Turk | furl | churn |
| | | | hurl | |

| -urse | -urt |
|-------|------|
| curse | curt |
| nurse | hurt |
| purse | blurt |
| | spurt |

**Purse**

# Phonics Patterns Diagnostic Test
**by Edward Fry, Ph.D.**

   This test will help the teacher quickly find the level of phonics development of any student, child or adult. Simply ask the student to read the nonsense word in each category below. Note on a separate sheet of paper or a copy of this test where errors are made, then teach the patterns in those categories. These categories (vowel sounds) match the categories in this Phonics Patterns book. There is an easy (or common) rhyme, or a harder (less common) rhyme in each nonsense word. If the student recognizes or knows the rhyme (vowel plus final consonant), he should be able to sound out each nonsense word.

|  | EASY PATTERNS | HARDER PATTERNS |
|---|---|---|
| Short A Sound | mab<br>fam | thasp<br>sance |
| Long A Sound | jace<br>baint | shaze<br>crange |
| Broad A Sound | dar<br>mard | tharge<br>narp |
| Short E Sound | jed<br>ket | threlp<br>betch |
| Long E Sound | ree<br>geat | smief<br>scheave |
| Short I Sound | pib<br>gligh | stisp<br>trinch |
| Long I Sound | pice<br>kile | drize<br>phie |
| Short O Sound | pob<br>bot | swomp<br>trox |
| Long O Sound | moe<br>goke | skown<br>flost |
| Short OO Sound | dook<br>tood | brould<br>froor |
| Long OO Sound | poot<br>mue | thew<br>floup |

|  | EASY PATTERNS | HARDER PATTERNS |
| --- | --- | --- |
| Broad O | nall<br>lork | choar<br>quawl |
| OI Sound | noil<br>croy | wroist<br>foin |
| OU Sound | jour<br>fout | shouse<br>kounce |
| Short U | pum<br>grunk | lotgh<br>sudge |
| UR Sound | hern<br>surn | zirl<br>slurse |

## Notes

It is not necessary to do the whole test in one sitting. Test a few categories, rest, teach to discovered needs, test more categories later.

Some vowel spellings can have more than one sound. For example, "EA" is a Short E in "great" and a Long E in "seat". Just explain that the same sound can be spelled different ways. Try to get the student to use the sound you are testing. As you teach these phonogram families, these different spellings (letters) for the same vowel sound will become readily apparent.

# Comprehensive Phonics Charts
## Phoneme – Grapheme Correspondence

## VOWEL SOUNDS (Alphabetical)

| Phoneme | | Common Spelling | Less Common Spelling |
|---|---|---|---|
| A Short | ă, a | A hat | |
| A Long | ā | A-E age, AI aid | EIGH eight, AY say, A (R) vary, AI (R) fair |
| A Broad | ä | A (R) far | A father |
| E Short | ě, e | E red | EA head, AI hair, A-E care |
| E Long | ē | E repay, EE see | EA seat, Y crazy |
| I Short | ĭ, i | I bit | Y gym |
| I Long | ī | I-E ice, Y try | I child, IE pie |
| O Short | ŏ, o | O hot | A watch |
| O Long | ō | O so, O-E nose | OA boat, OW know |
| O Broad | ô | O (R) for, O loss | A (L) all, A (U) auto, A (w) awful |
| OI Sound | oi | OI boil, OY boy | |
| OU Sound | ou | OU out, OW owl | |
| OO Long | o͞o, ü | OO moon | U ruby, EW chew, O do, OU soup, U-E duke |
| OO Short | o͝o, ú | OO good | U (L) pull, OU could |
| U Short | ŭ, ∂, u | U nut | O son |
| U Long | ū, yo͞o | U-E use, U music | |
| Schwa | ∂ | A alone, E taken, I direct, O onion, U circus | |
| Schwa + R | ∂r, ėr | ER her, IR sir, UR fur | |

(Some dictionaries say the schwa phoneme is the unaccented vowel sound, so it must be a polysyllable word. Other dictionaries say that schwa and short U are the same.)

## VOWEL SOUNDS (Clustered)

### Short Vowels

a - at    /ă/
e - end   /ĕ/
i - is    /ĭ/
o - hot   /ŏ/
u - up    /ŭ/

### Long Vowels
Open Syllable Rule

a - baby   /ā/
e - we     /ē/
i - idea   /ī/
o - so     /ō/

### Long Vowels
Final E Rule

a - make /ā/
e - here /ē/
i - five   /ī/
o - home /ō/
u - use   /ū/ or /yōō/

### Long Vowel
Digraphs

ai - aid   /ā/
ay - say   /ā/
ea - eat   /ē/
ee - see   /ē/
oa - oat   /ō/
ow - own   /ō/

### Schwa

a - principal /ə/
e - happen /ə/
o - action   /ə/

### Vowel Y

y - try, cycle /ī/
y - funny   /ē/

### Vowel Plus R

er - her   /ər/
ir - sir   /ər/
ur - fur   /ər/
ar - far   /är/
ar - vary  /ār/
or - for   /ôr/

### Dipthongs

oi - oil   /oi/
oy - hoy   /oi/
ou - out   /ou/
ow - how   /ou/

### Double O

oo - soon   /ōō/
oo - good   /ŏŏ/
u - truth   /ōō/
u - put     /ŏŏ/

### Broad O

o - long    /ô/
a (l) - also   /ô/
a (w) - saw /ô/
a (u) - auto /ô/

---

## Vowel Exceptions

ea - read    /ĕ/ or /ē/    "ea" makes both a long and a short E sound.

e (silent) - come, make    E at the end of a word is usually silent and sometimes makes the preceding vowel long.

y - yes    /y/    y is a consonant at the beginning of a word. (yes)
y is long I in a one syllable word or middle. (cycle) (by)
y is long E at the end of a polysyllable word. (funny)

le - candle   /əl/    final LE makes a schwa plus L sound.
al - pedal    /əl/    final AL makes a schwa plus L sound also.
ul - awful    /əl/    final UL makes a schwa plus L sound also.

## CONSONANT SOUNDS (Alphabetical)

| Phoneme | Common Spelling | Less Common Spelling |
| --- | --- | --- |
| B | B boy | |
| [C] | (No "C" phoneme; see K & S) | |
| CH | CH cheese | T nature |
| D | D dog | |
| F | F fat | PH phone |
| G | G girl | |
| H | H hot | |
| J | J just | |
| K | C cat, K king | CK sick, CH chrome |
| KS (blend) | X fox (No "X" phoneme) | |
| KW (blend) | QU quick (No "Q" phoneme) | |
| L | L look | |
| M | M me | |
| N | N no | KN knife |
| NG | NG sing | |
| P | P put | |
| [Q] | (No "Q" phoneme; see KW) | |
| R | R run | WR write |
| S | S sit, C city | |
| SH | SH shut, TI action | |
| T | T toy | |
| TH (voiced) | TH this | |
| TH (voiceless) | TH thing | |
| V | V voice | |
| W | W will | |
| WH | WH white / hw/ | |
| [X] | (No "X" phoneme; see KS) | |
| Y (consonant) | Y yes | I onion |
| Z | S is Z zero | |
| ZH | SI vision | S pleasure |

Note: Letters CH, NG, SH, TH, and WH are digraphs (two letters that make one phoneme). Letters KS and KW are blends, they are only included to help avoid confusion about the uses of letters X and Q.

# Comprehensive Phonics Charts, con't.

## CONSONANT SOUNDS (Clustered)

### Single Consonants

| | | | |
|---|---|---|---|
| b | h | n | v |
| c | j | p | w |
| d | k | r | y |
| f | l | s | z |
| g | m | t | |

### Important Exceptions

qu = / kw/ blend as in "quick"
(the letter "q" is never used without "u")
ph = / f/ sound as in "phone"
c = / s/ before i, e, or y, as in "city"
c = / k/ before a, o, or u, as in "cat"
g = / j/ before i, e, or y, as in "gem"
g = / g/ before a, o, or u, as in "good"
x = / ks/ blend as in "fox"
s = / z/ sound at the end of some words as in "is"
ng = / ng/ unique phoneme, as in "sing"
ck = / k/ often at end of word, as in "back"
(Note there is no "c" sound, no "q" sound
and no "x" sound.)

### Consonant Digraphs

**ch** as in "church"
**sh** as in "shoe"
**th** (voiced) as in "thin"
**th** (voiceless) as in "this"
**wh** (hw blend) as in "which"

### Rare Exceptions

ch = / k/ as in "character"
ch = / sh/ as in "chef"
ti = / sh/ as in "attention"
s = / sh/ as in "sure"
x = / gz/ as in "exact"
s = / zh/ as in "measure"
si = / zh/ as in "vision"

### Silent Consonants

gn = / n/ as in gnat"
kn = / n/ as in "knife"
wr = / r/ as in "write"
gh = / -/ as in "right"
mb = / m/ as in "lamb"
lf = / f/ as in "calf"
lk = / k/ as in "walk"
tle = / l/ as in "castle"
sc = / s/ as in "scent"

### Beginning Consonant Blends

| (r family) | (l family) | (s letter) | (s family) | (no family) |
|---|---|---|---|---|
| br | bl | sc | scr | dw |
| cr | cl | sk | squ | tw |
| dr | fl | sm | str | thr |
| fr | gl | sn | spr | |
| gr | pl | sp | spl | |
| pr | sl | st | shr | |
| tr | | sw | sch | |
| wr | | | | |

### Final Consonant Blends

*Note: These are usually best learned as part of rhymes.*

| | | | |
|---|---|---|---|
| ct - act | mp - jump | nt - ant | rk - dark |
| ft - lift | nc(e) - since | pt - kept | rt - art |
| ld - old | nd - and | rd - hard | st - least |
| lt - salt | nk - ink | | sk - risk |

# 100 Instant Words

We are certainly in favor of phonics instruction for helping beginning readers and writers improve their skills. There is, however, more to good reading and good spelling than phonics. Here is a list of the first 100 Instant Words. These are the most common words in English. In fact, it is nearly impossible to write a paragraph without using some of them. Because these 100 words make up half of all the words used in written English, they must be recognized (read) and written (spelled correctly) with little effort or hesitation. Note that many are not phonetically regular. Teach them as whole words, using flashcards, spelling lessons, or bingo games. If you want more Instant Words, see our publications 1000 Instant Words, or Spelling Book, Words Most Needed Plus Phonics for Grades 1-6 (3,000 Instant Words) listed inside the back cover.

| 1-5 | 16-20 | 31-35 |
|------|--------|--------|
| the | as | but |
| of | with | not |
| and | his | what |
| a | they | all |
| to | I | were |

| 6-10 | 21-25 | 36-40 |
|-------|--------|--------|
| in | at | we |
| is | be | when |
| you | this | your |
| that | have | can |
| it | from | said |

| 11-15 | 26-30 | 41-45 |
|--------|--------|--------|
| he | or | there |
| was | one | use |
| for | had | an |
| on | by | each |
| are | word | which |

| 46-50 | 66-70 | 86-90 |
|-------|-------|-------|
| she | him | call |
| do | into | who |
| how | time | oil |
| their | has | now |
| if | look | find |

| 51-55 | 71-75 | 91-95 |
|-------|-------|-------|
| will | two | long |
| up | more | down |
| other | write | day |
| about | go | did |
| out | see | get |

| 56-60 | 76-80 | 96-100 |
|-------|-------|--------|
| many | number | come |
| then | no | made |
| them | way | may |
| these | could | part |
| so | people | over |

| 61-65 | 81-85 |
|-------|-------|
| some | my |
| her | than |
| would | first |
| make | water |
| like | been |

# Index of Rhyme Patterns

## A

ab 12
ace 16
ack 12
act 12
ad 12
ade 16
aff 12
aft 12
ag 13
age 16
aid 16
ail 16
ain 16
aint 16
air 20
aise 16
ait 17
ake 17
ale 17
alf 43
alk 43
all 43
alt 43
am 13
ame 17
amp 13
an 13
ance 13
anch 13
and 13
ane 17
ang 14
ange 17
ank 14
ant 14
ap 14
ape 17
ar 19
ard 19
are 20
arge 19
ark 19
arl 19
arm 19
arn 19
arp 19
art 19
ase 17
ash 14
ask 14
asm 14
asp 15
ass 15
ast 15
aste 18
at 15
atch /a/ 15
    /ä/ 19
ate 18
ath 15

aught 43
ault 43
aunch 43
aunt 43
ave 18
aw 43
awl 43
awn 44
ax 15
ay 18
aze 18

## E

e 24
ea 24
each 24
ead /e/ 20
    /ē/ 24
eak /ā/ 18
    /ē/ 24
eal 24
ealth 20
eam 24
ean 24
eap 24
ear /e/ 20
    /ē/ 24
earn 53
ease 25
east 25
eat 25
eath /e/ 20
    /ē/ 25
eave 25
eck 20
ed 20
edge 21
ee 25
eech 25
eed 25
eef 25
eek 25
eel 26
eem 26
een 26
eep 26
eer 26
eet 26
eeze 26
eft 21
eg 21
eigh 18
eld 21
elf 21
ell 21
elp 21
elt 21
em 21
en 22
ence 22
ench 22

end 22
ength 22
ense 22
ent 22
ep 22
ept 22
erb 53
erge 53
erk 53
erm 53
ern 53
erve 53
esh 22
ess 23
est 23
et 23
etch 23
ew 40
ex 23
ext 23
ey 18

## I

ib 27
ibe 31
ice 31
ick 27
id 27
ide 31
idge 27
ie 31
iece 26
ied 31
ief 26
ield 26
ier 31
ies 31
ife 31
iff 27
ift 27
ig 27
igh 31
ight 31, 32
ike 32
ild 32
ile 32
ilk 27
ill 28
ilt 28
im 28
ime 32
imp 28
in 28
ince 28
inch 28
ind 32
ine 32
ing 29
inge 29
ink 29
int 29

ip 29
ipe 32
ir 53
ird 53
ire 33
irk 53
irl 54
irst 54
irt 54
irth 54
is 29
ise 33
ish 29
isk 30
isp 30
iss 30
ist 30
it 30
itch 30
ite 33
ive /i/ 30
    /ī/ 33
ix 30
ize 33

## O

o /ō/ 36
    /ü/ 40
oach 36
oad 36
oak 36
oal 36
oam 36
oan 36
oar 44
oast 36
oat 36
ob 34
obe 36
ock 34
od 34
ode 37
oe 37
oft 34
og 34
ogue 37
oice 46
oil 46
oin 46
oint 46
oise 46
oist 46
oke 37
old 37
ole 37
oll /o/ 34
    /ō/ 37
olt 37
ome /ō/ 37
    /u/ 49
omp 34

on 49
ond 34
one /ō/ 37
    /u/ 49
ong 44
ont 38
oo 40
ood /ù/ 39
    /ü/ 40
oof 40
ook 39
ool 40
oom 40
oon 40
oop 40
oor /ù/ 39
    /ô/ 44
oose 41
oot /ù/ 39
    /ü/ 41
ooth 41
ooze 41
op 35
ope 38
orch 44
ord 44
ore 44
ork 44
orm 44
orn 45
ort 45
ose /ō/ 38
    /o͞o/ 41
oss 45
ost /ō/ 38
    /ô/ 45
ot 35
otch 35
ote 38
oth 45
ouch 47
oud 47
ough/o/ 35
    /u/ 49
ought 45
ould 39
ounce 47
ound 47
ount 47
oup 41
our /ô/ 45
    /ou/ 47
ouse 47
out 47
outh 47

ove /ō/ 38
    /u/ 49
ow /ō/ 38
    /ou/ 48
owl 48
own /ō/ 38

    /ou/ 48
owse 48
ox 35
oy 46

## U

ub 49
ube 41
uce 41
uch 49
uck 49
ud 50
ude 41
udge 50
ue 41
uff 50
ug 50
uke 42
ule 42
ulk 50
ull /ù/ 39
    /u/ 50
um 50
umb 50
ume 42
ump 51
un 51
unch 51
une 42
ung 51
unk 51
unt 51
up 51
ur 54
urb 54
ure 42
urge 54
urk 54
url 54
urn 54
urse 54
urt 54
us 51
use 42
ush /ù/ 39
    /u/ 52
usk 52
uss 52
ust 52
ut 52
utch 52
ute 42
uth 42
utt 52
uy 33

y 33
ye 33

# Suggested Teaching Order

Which rhymes do you teach first?  Here's one suggestion based on the number of examples of rhymes appearing in this book.

| **RHYME** | **EXAMPLES** | | | | |
|-----------|--------------|---|---|---|---|
| -ay | jay | say | pay | day | play |
| -ill | hill | Bill | will | fill | spill |
| -ip | ship | dip | tip | skip | trip |
| -at | cat | fat | bat | rat | sat |
| -am | ham | jam | dam | ram | Sam |
| -ag | bag | rag | tag | wag | sag |
| -ack | back | sack | Jack | black | track |
| -ank | bank | sank | tank | blank | drank |
| -ick | sick | Dick | pick | quick | chick |
| -ell | bell | sell | fell | tell | yell |
| -ot | pot | not | hot | dot | got |
| -ing | ring | sing | king | wing | thing |
| -ap | cap | map | tap | clap | trap |
| -unk | sunk | junk | bunk | flunk | skunk |
| -ail | pail | jail | nail | sail | tail |
| -ain | rain | pain | main | chain | plain |
| -eed | feed | seed | weed | need | freed |
| -y | my | by | dry | try | fly |
| -out | pout | trout | scout | shout | spout |
| -ug | rug | bug | hug | dug | tug |
| -op | mop | cop | pop | top | hop |
| -in | pin | tin | win | chin | thin |
| -an | pan | man | ran | tan | Dan |
| -est | best | nest | pest | rest | test |
| -ink | pink | sink | rink | link | drink |
| -ow | low | slow | grow | show | snow |
| -ew | new | few | chew | grew | blew |
| -ore | more | sore | tore | store | score |
| -ed | bed | red | fed | led | Ted |
| -ab | cab | dab | jab | lab | crab |
| -ob | cob | job | rob | Bob | knob |
| -ock | sock | rock | lock | dock | block |
| -ake | cake | lake | make | take | brake |
| -ine | line | nine | pine | fine | shine |
| -ight | knight | light | right | night | fight |
| -im | swim | him | Kim | rim | brim |
| -uck | duck | luck | suck | truck | buck |
| -um | gum | bum | hum | drum | plum |